THE
VERY LUCKY
SYLLABLE
TYPES

PHONICS READ-ALOUDS

Title: The Very Lucky Syllable Types
ISBN: 9798312563344
First Published in the United States of America, 2025

Contributors: Manns, Yvette, author; Blu, Ana K., illustrator

Summary: The consonants and vowels find a magical clover in the field that teaches them about syllable types. They learn about closed, consonant+le, open, vowel team, silent e and r controlled syllables, along with unstressed syllables that have a schwa sound.

www.PhonicsReadAlouds.com

THE
VERY LUCKY
SYLLABLE
TYPES

Written by: Yvette Manns
Illustrated by: Ana K. Blu

It was the top of the morning in March, and the letters were gathered in the field to do their word building tasks. A, G, I, U, and X were buzzing with excitement and pointing above their heads. C approached the letters to ask what they were clamoring about.

"Look up there! There's a rainbow in the sky!"
L shouted. "We should see if there is a pot of gold
at the end of it." The letters ran across the field to
search for what was at the end of the rainbow.
"Over here! I see something glowing!" X shouted.

When they reached the end of the rainbow, there wasn't a pot of gold, but something shiny caught their attention. They raced to the spot and found...

...a sparkling clover shimmering in the field!

This was no regular clover; it was a clover with different colors on the edge of each leaf. O said, "I've heard of a lucky four-leaf clover, but this one must be extra special because it has six different colors on its leaves."

"Hi, I'm Chloe, the Syllable Clover, and each of my leaves represents a syllable type. If you can learn them, I will help you build longer words."

"What's a syllable?" X asked.
Chloe answered, "A syllable is a word or a word part with a vowel sound. For example, in the word 'clover,' there are two syllables — clo/ver."

"I've been growing in the field, patiently waiting for you to be ready to learn about different syllable types," Chloe explained. "Before I can teach you, you should invite a few friends. We'll need Bossy R, Schwa, and Silent E."

When Bossy R, Schwa, and Silent E arrived, the consonants and vowels welcomed them with open arms.
"I see we are at the end of a rainbow. Did you bring me here to finally get my missing gold?" Bossy R asked.

Chloe answered, "Sorry, Bossy R. A leprechaun left with the pot of gold an hour ago, but I know you will 'treasure' what I have to share with you."

"I'm going to explain all my leaves and the different types of syllables," Chloe continued.

Closed

"My blue leaf has a C on it. The C stands for 'closed,' which means that a syllable ends with a consonant and the vowel is short, like in the words 'rabbit' and 'pot.'

"My orange leaf has the letter L on it, which shows that these syllable types end in a consonant, then an -le. The words 'pebble' and 'sprinkle' end with a syllable that ends in consonant +le."

consonant +LE

Open

"The red leaf with an O on it represents open syllables, which means it ends with a vowel, and the vowel's sound is long, like in the first syllable in the word 'tiger' or both syllables in 'halo.'

"My pink leaf has a V on it that stands for Vowel Team. Any time there are two vowels that represent one sound or a diphthong, this falls in the Vowel Team type. The word 'daydream' has vowel teams in both syllables.

Vowel Team

Silent E

"The gray leaf with an E on it stands for a syllable with a Silent E at the end. The words 'home' and 'compete' have Silent E syllables."

"My purple leaf has an R on it, and that stands for R-controlled syllables. The vowel and the R must be in the same syllable, like in the words 'turtle' and 'dart.'

R-Controlled

morn

ing

Bossy R remarked, "Arr, I was expecting gold at the end of the rainbow, but this was pretty good too!"

Chloe explained, "Different syllable types can combine to build multisyllabic words like the word 'morning'. R-controlled and closed are the two syllable types that create that word."

C commented, "The syllable types are so cool!"

Chloe beamed. "Now it's time to practice what you've learned!" They built words with the syllable types.

shamrock   tulip   rainbow
wiggle   milkshake   turtle

Chloe explained, "Schwa, you are a part of a special category. Some syllables have a schwa or other patterns, like at the end of the words, 'cabbage' or 'station.' My stem is yellow, just for you and the others! You also represent the sound in the middle syllable in the word 'leprechaun!'

cabbage   station   leprechaun

Silent E mentioned, "I notice I'm at the end of two syllable types — c+LE and Silent E."
Chloe explained, "Yes! Most syllables have a written vowel, even if it does not represent a sound. Only a few words, such as 'prism' and 'rhythm,' don't have a written vowel in both syllables."

"Well, Chloe," C said. "You taught us all about the types of syllables and longer words. We welcome you to stay around as long as you want so we can keep building words with different syllable types. How do you feel about that?"

TIPS FOR AFTER READING

- Go on a word hunt and find all the words in this story with more than one syllable.
- Sort the words you find by the syllable type and share with a classmate.
- Read all the words in each syllable type out loud.
- Draw Chloe the Syllable Clover and write one word in each syllable type on her leaves and stem.
- Using another passage or text, highlight all the multisyllabic words you can find.

FUN FACTS ABOUT SYLLABLE TYPES

- There are six main syllable types and some syllables are leftovers that include schwa, and some prefixes and suffixes.
- Closed syllables are the most common syllables that we read in words.
- Every syllable must have a vowel sound.
- Multisyllabic words are words that have more than one syllable, such as "clover" (2) and "leprechaun" (3).
- Words with a closed syllable have a short vowel sound and words with an open syllable have a long vowel sound.
- Some multisyllabic words can have a syllable that is unstressed and have a schwa sound in place of the long vowel. For example: "basket," "other," "pelican," and "alphabet."
- Here are some more words that are made up of different syllable types:

> bumble flower garden lemon music nation
> pancake paper rainy spider sunset tremble winter

CAN YOU THINK OF ANY MORE WORDS WITH DIFFERENT SYLLABLE TYPES?

CHECK OUT OTHER BOOKS IN THE SERIES!

...and more books!

STAY IN THE KNOW!

Visit
www.PhonicsReadAlouds.com
for activities, stickers, and more!

DID YOU ENJOY THIS STORY?

★★★★★

Please consider leaving us a review on Amazon. This helps us to learn what you want to read about next and tell other people about our stories!

 PhonicsReadAlouds  PhonicsReadAlouds  PhonicsReadAlouds

Made in the USA
Coppell, TX
12 July 2025

51749836R00017